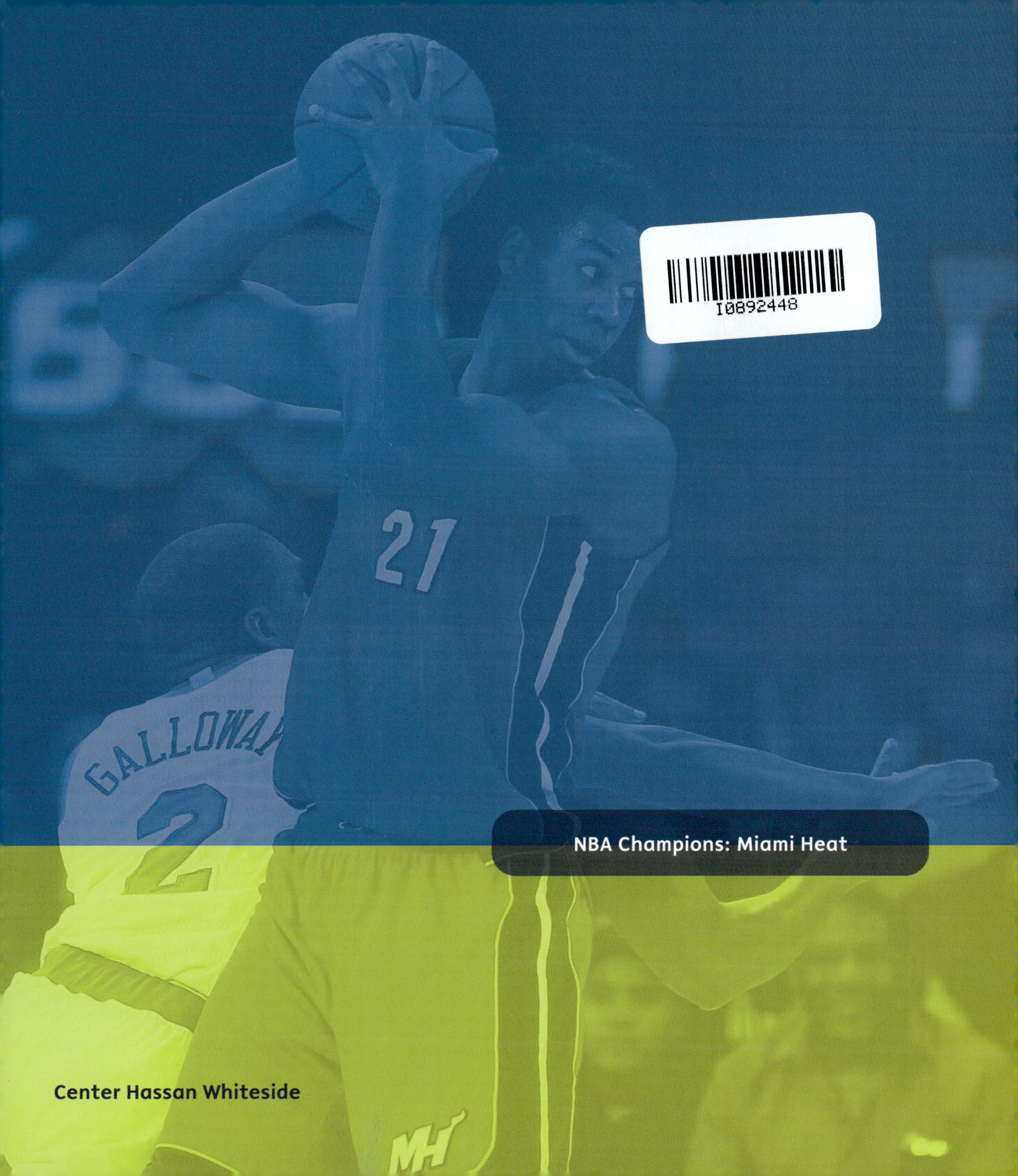

NBA Champions: Miami Heat

Center Hassan Whiteside

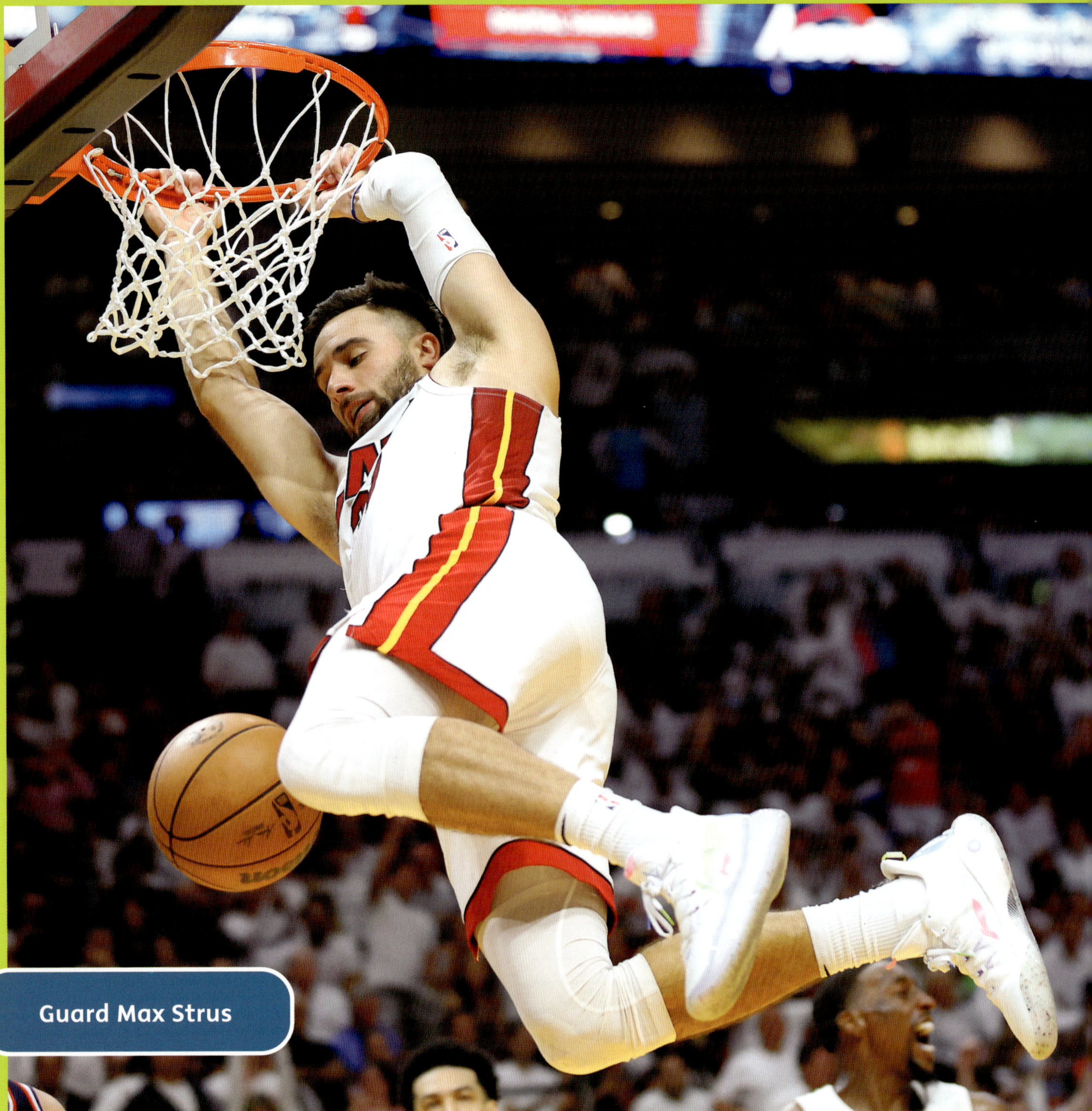

Guard Max Strus

NBA CHAMPIONS

MIAMI HEAT

BY JAMES BARRY

CREATIVE EDUCATION / CREATIVE PAPERBACKS

Forward LeBron James

Published by Creative Education and Creative Paperbacks
P.O. Box 227, Mankato, Minnesota 56002
Creative Education and Creative Paperbacks are imprints of
The Creative Company
www.thecreativecompany.us

Art Direction by Tom Morgan
Book production by Graham Morgan
Edited by Grace Cain

Images by Associated Press/Toby Massey, 15; HANS DERYK/Reuters, 4; Getty Images/Andrew D. Bernstein, 6, 7, David Berding, cover, Fernando Medina, 12, Issac Baldizon, cover, 16, Jamie Squire, 19, Jason Miller, 20, Jim McIsaac, 1, 10, John W. McDonough, 5, Michael Reaves, 2, Mike Ehrmann, 3, Peter Llewellyn, 24; Unsplash/Muzammil Soorma, 9
Every effort has been made to contact copyright holders for material reproduced in this book. Any omissions will be rectified in subsequent printings if notice is given to the publisher.

Library of Congress Cataloging-in-Publication Data

Names: Barry, James (author of children's books), author.
Title: Miami Heat / by James Barry.
Description: Mankato, Minnesota : Creative Education and Creative Paperbacks, [2025] | Series: Creative Sports: NBA champions | ATOS: 3.7. | Audience: Ages 7-10 years | Audience: Grades 2-3 | Summary: "Elementary-level text and dynamic sports photos highlight the NBA championship wins of the Miami Heat, plus sensational players associated with the professional basketball team such as Jimmy Butler"— Provided by publisher.
Identifiers: LCCN 2024014659 (print) | LCCN 2024014660 (ebook) | ISBN 9798889892595 (library binding) | ISBN 9781682776254 (paperback) | ISBN 9798889893707 (ebook)
Subjects: LCSH: Miami Heat (Basketball team)—Juvenile literature. | Basketball—Florida—Miami—Juvenile literature.
Classification: LCC GV885.52.M53 B37 2025 (print) | LCC GV885.52.M53 (ebook) | DDC 796.323/6409759381—dc23/eng/20240418
LC record available at https://lccn.loc.gov/2024014659
LC ebook record available at https://lccn.loc.gov/2024014660

Printed in China

Coach Pat Riley

Forward LeBron James

CONTENTS

Home of the Heat

Miami, Florida, is famous for warm beaches and music with a beat. It is also home to an **arena** called the Kaseya Center. A basketball team called the Heat plays there.

Guard Dwyane Wade

The Miami Heat are part of the National Basketball Association (NBA). They play in the Southeast Division. That's part of the Eastern Conference. Their **rivals** include the Boston Celtics and the New York Knicks. All NBA teams want to win the **NBA Finals** and become champions.

Center Alonzo Mourning

Naming the Heat

Team owners held a contest to find a good name. Three of the top picks were Waves, Sharks, and Heat. The owners decided on Heat. It fit the sunny weather in Miami. They also hoped the team would be a hot winner!

Heat History

The Heat began playing in 1988. They started slowly. The team only won 15 games in its first season. The next year, high-scoring forward Glen Rice joined the Heat. They started to improve.

In 1995, Pat Riley became the Heat's head coach and team president. He added key players. They traded for shot-blocking center Alonzo Mourning. Tricky guard Tim Hardaway came too. The two stars led the Heat to the **playoffs** six years in a row.

Center Skip Thoren

Guard Dwayne Wade

In 2003, the Heat made a great decision. They chose slick guard Dwyane Wade in the NBA Draft. He became one of the best Heat players ever. In 2006, Wade and powerful center Shaquille O'Neal led the Heat to their first NBA championship!

In 2010, superstar forward LeBron James joined Wade. So did high-scoring center and power forward Chris Bosh. The three stars led the Heat to the Finals four years in a row. Miami won two more **titles**.

Other Heat Stars

Over the years, the Heat have had many good players. Center Rony Seikaly was a strong **rebounder**. **Swingman** Eddie Jones was a top scorer in the early 2000s.

Power forward Udonis Haslem was one of the Heat's best rebounders for many years. He grabbed the most rebounds in team history.

Swingman Eddie Jones

Forward Jimmy Butler

Point guard Goran Dragić was a great passer. He was an **all-star** with the Heat.

Forward Jimmy Butler and center-forward Bam Adebayo are the Heat's best players today. They've led Miami to the Finals twice in the 2020s. Will head coach Erik Spoelstra and his two stars win the team its fourth championship? Heat fans surely hope so!

About the Heat

First season: 1988–89

Conference/division: Eastern Conference, Southeast Division

Team colors: black, red, and yellow

Home arena: Kaseya Center

NBA CHAMPIONSHIPS:

2006, 4 games to 2 over Dallas Mavericks

2012, 4 games to 1 over Oklahoma City Thunder

2013, 4 games to 3 over San Antonio Spurs

TEAM WEBSITE:

https://www.nba.com/heat

Glossary

all-star—a player picked to play in the All-Star Game, featuring the season's top stars

arena—a large building with seats for spectators, where sports games and entertainment events are held

NBA Finals—a series of games between two teams at the end of the playoffs; the first team to win four games is the champion

playoffs—games that the best teams play after a regular season to see who the champion will be

rebounder—a player who catches and controls the ball after a missed shot

rival—a team that plays extra hard against another team

swingman—a basketball player who can play guard or forward

title—another word for championship

Guard Josh Richardson

Index